We want to learn First German

Written by Nicola Baxter

Illustrated by Belinda Lyon

Learning German

Learning a new language is fun. It's like breaking a secret code and the more you do it, the easier it gets. Like any code, a language has rules. You don't need to worry about these too much to begin with, but here are a few things you need to know.

Speaking German

Words like bus, sofa and baby are spelt the same as in English, but they are said in a German way. Ask someone to show you how to say the words in this book.

German nouns

The first thing you will notice about German is that there are a lot of capital letters. In English a word that is the name of a person or a town or a country begins with a capital letter. In German *all* names of things begin with a capital letter. They are called nouns.

In English there is only one word for *the*. We say:

the tree

the flag

the house

But in German there are three different words for *the*.

der Baum

die Flagge

das Haus

As you learn each noun, try to remember which word for *the* goes with it.

The word for *a* or *an* or *one* is *ein* or *eine*. You can tell which if you know whether the noun goes with *der, die* or *das*.

ein Baum   eine Flagge   ein Haus

Plurals

When we want to talk about more than one thing, we use the plural of the noun. In English this usually means that we add an s. German nouns form their plurals in several different ways. Don't worry too much about this but try to learn them when you come across them. There is a list of all the plurals of the German words in this book at the back.

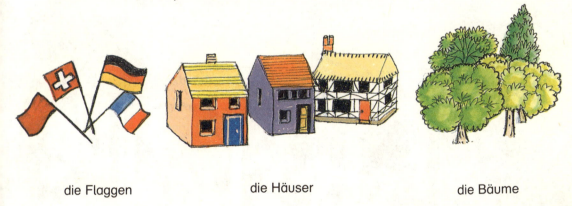

die Flaggen   die Häuser   die Bäume

They all use the same word for *the*, though.

Special signs

The little marks over some of the letters, as in the words above, warn you that the sound has changed. You will find out how as you learn to say the words.

German has one letter that we don't have in English: ß.
It stands for the sound *ss*.

Wieviel Kinder?
How many children?

ein Kind

---- Kinder

--- Kind?

Wie alt bist du?
How old are you?

Ich bin zwei Jahre alt.

Ich bin zehn Jahre alt.

Ich bin fünf Jahre alt.

Wer ist das?
Who is this?

Das ist meine Schwester.

Das ist mein Vater.

Das ist meine ----------.

Das ist mein ------.

Hast du Geschwister?
Do you have brothers and sisters?

Ich habe vier Schwestern.

Ich habe einen Bruder.

Was ist das?
What is this?

Das ist ein Kleid.

Das sind Hausschuhe.

Das sind ------.

Das ist ein ----.

Die Farben

blau

rot

grün

gelb

braun

schwarz

orange

rosa

weiß

grau

Welche Farbe ist der Hut?
What colour is the hat?

Der Hut ist ------- und ----.

Der Hut ist ------.

Der Hut ist blau.

Der Hut ist ----.

Welche Farbe ist der Schal?
What colour is the scarf?

Der Schal ist grau und rosa
und orange
und braun
und grün
und rot
und blau
und gelb
und schwarz
und weiß!

Was ist das?

Das ist eine Brille.

Das ist ein Buch.

Das ist ein ----.

Das ist ein ------.

Die Hobbies

tanzen

malen

Fußball spielen

fernsehen

lesen

schwimmen

Was machst du gern?
What do you like doing?

Ich tanze gern.

Ich tanze nicht gern.

Ich spiele gern Fußball.

Ich ---- nicht gern.

Ich -------- nicht gern.

Malst du gern?
Do you like painting?

Nein!   Ja!

Wie ist das Wetter?
What is the weather like?

Es ist schön.

Es ist kalt.

Es ist nebelig.

Es ist windig.

Es ist heiß.

Es regnet.

Es schneit.

Die Jahreszeiten

Im Winter ist es ----.

Im Sommer ist es heiß.

Im Herbst ist es ------.

Im Frühling ist es -----.

Word list

Plurals are given in brackets after their nouns. If there is no word in brackets, the plural of the noun does not change. Remember plurals all use the same word for *the*: die.

acht *eight*
der Anorak (Anoraks) *anorak*
das Auto (Autos) *car*

das Baby (Babies) *baby*
der Ball (Bälle) *ball*
die Bank (Bänke) *bench*
der Bauernhof (Bauernhöfe) *farm*
der Baum (Bäume) *tree*
der Berg (Berge) *mountain*
das Bild (Bilder) *picture*
blau *blue*
der Bleistift (Bleistifte) *pencil*
die Blume (Blumen) *flower*
braun *brown*
die Brille (Brillen) *glasses*
die Brücke (Brücken) *bridge*
der Bruder (Brüder) *brother*
das Bücherregal (Bücherregale) *bookcase*
das Buch (Bücher) *book*
der Bürgersteig (Bürgersteige) *pavement*
der Bus (Busse) *bus*

das Café (Cafés) *café*

das Dach (Dächer) *roof*
die Dame (Damen) *lady*
das Dorf (Dörfer) *village*
drei *three*

ein, eine *one*
die Ente (Enten) *duck*
es *it*

die Fabrik (Fabriken) *factory*
das Fahrrad (Fahrräder) *bicycle*
die Familie (Familien) *family*
die Farbe (Farben) *colour*
der Farbkasten (Farbkästen) *paintbox*
das Feld (Felder) *field*
das Fenster *window*
fernsehen *to watch television*
der Fernseher *television*
die Flagge (Flaggen) *flag*
der Fluß (Flüsse) *river*
das Foto (Fotos) *photograph*

der Frühling *spring*
Fußball spielen *to play football*
fünf *five*

der Garten (Gärten) *garden*
gelb *yellow*
das Geschäft (Geschäfte) *shop*
die Geschwister *brothers and sisters*
grau *grey*
die Großmutter (Großmütter) *grandmother*
der Großvater (Großväter) *grandfather*
grün *green*
der Gürtel *belt*

ich habe *I have*
der Handschuh (Handschuhe) *glove*
das Haus (Häuser) *house*
der Hausschuh (Hausschuhe) *slipper*
das Heft (Hefte) *notebook*
heiß *hot*
der Heizkörper *radiator*
das Hemd (Hemden) *shirt*
der Herbst *autumn*
der Herr (Herren) *gentleman*
das Hobby (Hobbys) *hobby*
die Hose (Hosen) *trousers*
das Hotel (Hotels) *hotel*
der Hügel *hill*
das Huhn (Hühner) *chicken*
der Hund (Hunde) *dog*
der Hut (Hüte) *hat*

ich *I*
ist *is*

das Jahr (Jahre) *year*
die Jahreszeit (Jahreszeiten) *season*
ja *yes*
die Jeans (plural) *jeans*
der Junge (Jungen) *boy*

der Kalender *calendar*
kalt *cold*
das Kaninchen *rabbit*
die Karte (Karten) *map*
die Katze (Katzen) *cat*
das Kind (Kinder) *child*
das Kissen *cushion*
der Klebstoff *glue*
die Kleidung (plural) *clothes*
das Kleid (Kleider) *dress*
kochen *to cook*
die Krawatte (Krawatten) *tie*
der Kugelschreiber *ballpoint pen*

die Kuh (Kühe) cow
die Lampe (Lampen) lamp
das Land (Länder) country
der Lastwagen lorry
die Lehrerin (Lehrerinnen) teacher
lesen to read
der Lieferwagen van
das Lineal (Lineale) ruler

das Mädchen girl
malen to paint
der Mantel (Mäntel) coat
mein my
der Morgenmantel (Morgenmäntel) dressing gown
das Motorrad (Motorräder) motorbike
die Mutter (Mütter) mother

nebelig foggy
nein no
das Nest (Nester) nest
neun nine
nicht not

orange orange

der Papierkorb (Papierkörbe) wastepaper bin
das Papier paper
der Pfad (Pfade) path
das Pferd (Pferde) horse
die Pflanze (Pflanzen) plant
der Pinsel paintbrush
der Pullover jumper

es regnet it is raining
der Rock (Röcke) skirt
rosa pink
rot red

die Schachtel cardboard box
das Schaf (Schafe) sheep
der Schal (Schals) scarf
die Schere (Scheren) scissors
der Schlafanzug (Schlafanzüge) pyjamas
der Schmetterling (Schmetterlinge) butterfly
es schneit it is snowing
schön fine
der Schornstein (Schornsteine) chimney
der Schrank (Schränke) cupboard
der Schuh (Schuhe) shoe
die Schule (Schulen) school
die Schultasche (Schultaschen) schoolbag
der Schultisch (Schultische) desk
schwarz black
das Schwein (Schweine) pig

die Schwester (Schwestern) sister
schwimmen to swim
sechs six
der Sessel armchair
sieben seven
der Slip (Slips) knickers
die Socke (Socken) sock
das Sofa (Sofas) sofa
der Sommer summer
die Sonne sun
das Spielzeug toy
die Straßenlaterne (Straßenlaternen) streetlight
die Stadt (Städte) town
der Stiefel boot
die Straße (Straßen) street, road
die Strumpfhose (Strumpfhosen) tights
der Stuhl (Stühle) chair

die Tafel (Tafeln) chalkboard
die Tankstelle (Tankstellen) petrol station
tanzen to dance
der Teich (Teiche) pond
der Teppich (Teppiche) carpet
der Tisch (Tische) table
der Traktor tractor
der Turnschuh (Turnschuhe) trainer
die Tür (Türen) door
das T-Shirt (T-Shirts) T-Shirt

die Uhr (Uhren) clock
und and

der Vater (Väter) father
vier four
der Vogel (Vögel) bird
der Vorhang (Vorhänge) curtain

der Wald (Wälder) forest
die Wand (Wände) wall
weiß white
wer who
das Wetter weather
wieviel how many
windig windy
der Winter winter
die Wohnung (Wohnungen) flat
das Wohnzimmer sitting room
der Wolkenkratzer skyscraper

die Zahl (Zahlen) number
zehn ten
die Zeichnung (Zeichnungen) drawing
die Zeitung (Zeitungen) newspaper
zwei two